W9-BED-302

jkjc

REMARKABLE PLANTS

CHALLENGE YOURSELF

WEIRD TRIVIA AND UNBELIEVABLE FACTS TO TEST YOUR KNOWLEDGE
ABOUT FLOWERS, FUNGI, ALGAE, & MORE!

JEFF PROBST

REMARKABLE PLANTS

CHALLENGE YOURSELF

Puffin Books

PUFFIN BOOKS
An imprint of Penguin Random House LLC
375 Hudson Street
New York, New York 10014

First published in the United States of America by Puffin Books,
an imprint of Penguin Random House LLC, 2017

LIBRARY OF CONGRESS CATALOGING-IN-PUBLICATION DATA IS AVAILABLE

ISBN 9780147518095 (hardcover)
ISBN 9780147518088 (paperback)

Printed in China

1 3 5 7 9 10 8 6 4 2

Designed by Maria Fazio

Photo Credits

Thinkstock: pages i–ii, iv (bottom two images), 41 (right column), 49 (top), 51, 62–63, 103,
108 (bottom two images), 115, 119, 124

Shutterstock: pages iv, 2–19, 20–21 24–47, 49–50, 52–61, 64–95, 97, 99, 100, 102–104,
107–114, 116–118, 122–123, 125–149, 150–151, 154–159

iStock: pages 22–23, 101, 149 (top left corner), 152–153

Wiki Commons: pages 120–121

All background patterns courtesy of Shutterstock: pages vi–1, 6–7, 10, 12–13, 16–19, 21–22,
24, 26–27, 32–35, 44–45, 48–50, 62–63, 66–71, 76–77, 80–89, 92–94, 96–98, 100–103,
106–114, 116, 118, 122–125, 130–133, 136, 138, 141, 144–145, 148, 151, 154–156

All other photos courtesy of the author

This book is dedicated to Amanda and Abby!
You are both amazing . . . and you make it *so much
fun* to be an uncle! It's been an honor watching
you grow into young women. I can't wait for our
next adventure together! I love you girls from
the salt to the pepper!

Uncle Jeff

Hey, young readers!

Here's a funny and slightly embarrassing piece of personal trivia. My very first job in television was as the host of a "home and garden" show that we shot in Seattle. I was supposed to be an expert as I explained how to plant and take care of various types of plants, flowers, grass, and anything else connected to gardening. The truth was I didn't know a thing! I just memorized what I was supposed to say and acted like I understood! Fake it till you make it, right?

So this book was a really fun opportunity for me to actually learn a few things about plants and other plant-like species such as fungi and lichen. I had NO IDEA how many different types of plants there are in the world. Now when I travel for *Survivor*, I look at everything much differently!

It's an awesome world, so much to learn!

I hope you enjoy the book!

Jeff Probst

Note to readers:
See a word in bold? Check out the glossary in the back to find out what it means.

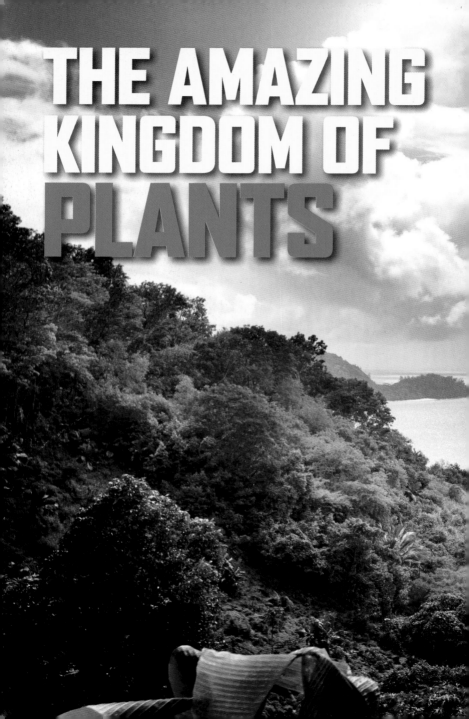

THE AMAZING KINGDOM OF PLANTS

Plants are living things that grow out of the earth and usually survive by absorbing nutrients through their roots. Almost all plants contain a substance called chlorophyll, which helps absorb the sunlight necessary to create food to sustain them. Grass, ferns, trees, flowers, moss, fruits, and vegetables are all examples of plants. There are countless varieties of plants around the world, and even some still waiting to be discovered!

SLIME!
POND SCUM!
SEAWEED!

ALGAE

Considered the ancient ancestors of modern plants, **algae** make up a huge amount of life on Earth (about half!) and can be found in nearly every known habitat. Algae are classified into major groups by color: green, brown, and red. There are also blue-green algae, which are actually a type of **bacteria**.

Like other plants, algae convert sunlight into food through a process called **photosynthesis**. But unlike most other plants, algae do not have roots, stems, or leaves.

There are something like 72,500 **species** of algae, ranging in size from microscopic pico-plankton to giant kelp, which can grow to be 160 feet or more—taller than the average tree!

CRAZY BUT TRUE

Scientists believe that algae produce 87% of the world's oxygen. They also help remove huge amounts of carbon dioxide from the atmosphere and serve as food for countless fish and other marine life.

ALGAE

Most **algae** are single-celled organisms. They drift alone in water or gather in colonies. Others form more plantlike shapes, including branching **filaments** or fronds.

Not all algae grow in water. Algae can be found on tree branches, in the soil, on damp bricks and stones—even on animals. Wild sloths, for example, let algae grow in their fur, using it as camouflage.

SLOTH

TRUE OR FALSE?
You probably have algae in your bathroom.

ANSWER: **True!** (Though hopefully it isn't growing there!) Used as makeup (rouge) in ancient Rome, algae are still used today to make lipstick, hand lotion, and other beauty products.

CRAZY BUT TRUE

Algae are found in toothpaste, too. The crushed husks of special algae called diatoms are the gritty polish you feel when brushing your teeth.

Diatoms are also found in metal polishes and dynamite! Pigments from other algae are used in food coloring, clothing dyes, and rubber.

toothpaste

7

Go, Seed, Go!

SURVIVAL OF A SPECIES

For most plants, having offspring is dependent on getting **seeds** out into the world. Many plants live for only one year, so there's no problem with them dropping seeds right where they are. But for plants that live multiple years, it's important that they spread seeds far and wide, so the parent plant doesn't have to compete with young ones for survival.

EXPLODING SEEDS!

Some plants have adapted ways to launch their **seeds**, flinging them in weird ways as far as they can. Mature pea pods, for example, dry in the sun until they suddenly split open. And when they do, the seeds spring out. Other plants, such as impatiens, grow pods that pop at the slightest touch, spraying seeds in all directions— like mines waiting to be triggered. Lupines, California poppies, pansies, violets, and many other plants all catapult their seeds outward in an attempt to claim new ground.

CALIFORNIA POPPIES

SANDBOX TREE

The spiny-trunked, poison-leafed sandbox tree is the most explosive of them all. Not only does it have dark spikes and toxic sap, but the tree's fruit explodes so loudly that it's been nicknamed the dynamite tree. And when it does explode, it shoots seeds at speeds up to 160 miles per hour!

The first primitive flowers appeared only 130 million years ago. They didn't have colorful petals or enticing smells yet. That came later. Still, flowers were a true game changer for the plant kingdom. Before then, all seed-producing plants were **gymnosperms**, which produce offspring by sending and receiving reproductive material through the air in the hit-or-miss process of wind **pollination**.

The development of flowers allowed plants to enlist insects and other animals to help in pollination, which requires less **pollen** and uses up less of a plant's energy. Flowering plants flourished, producing an incredible diversity of new **species** in a relatively short amount of time.

Coast redwoods, bristlecone pines, ginkgo trees, and even Christmas trees are all part of the group of plants called gymnosperms. The name comes from Greek words meaning "naked seeds," because unlike most other seed-producing plants (called **angiosperms**), these plants have no flowers and produce no fruit.

BRISTLECONE PINE

GINKGO TREE

DIVERSITY IN BLOOM

Petals made a huge difference in the ability of flowering plants to survive. Since petals serve as advertisements for flowers, visually telling insects where the flowers are, the adaptation gave some plants a distinct advantage. Using scent, petals could also attract pollinators far out of view—including miles away.

Thanks to flowers, **angiosperms** began to dominate the landscape. Canopy-forming trees replaced **primordial** conifers, transforming entire ecosystems.

Today, there are roughly 235,000 known **species** of flowering plants. Combined, they outnumber non-flowering plants 20 to 1!

The Art of Attraction

Plants and insects evolved together, with some insects adapting to see or smell or drink nectar better than others. Over time, flowering plants developed mutually beneficial relationships with insects, providing blooms that attracted one specific pollinator.

Some plants learned to mimic the traits of others. The Fringed Leek orchid, for example, looks remarkably similar to a flower that provides nectar to ants, even though it has no nectar to give. But by the time the insect figures out the trick, the job of **pollination** is already done.

The comet orchid of Madagascar stores its nectar inside a long spine jutting out the back of the flower. The spine is so long, only the tongue of a specific insect—the hawk moth—can reach it.

HAWK MOTH

GUSTAVIA

One of the cool things I learned on location in the Amazon rain forest is that a variety of the plant Gustavia has flowers that, once open, release their pollen only when they "hear" a specific musical note—one made by a specific type of night-flying sweat bee when it buzzes.

StRaNGE PoLLiNAToRS

Since most cacti bloom at night, they require the help of unusual pollinators— bats!

BATS

While most insects are attracted to sweet smells, bats are attracted to the scent of rotting fruit. Many cactus flowers have a similar smell.

CACTUS FRUIT

Some bats rely on cactus flowers to cross the desert as much as cacti rely on bats for **pollination**. These flying mammals survive their travels by drinking nectar on the way to their breeding grounds.

And then, on the way back, they're able to eat the fruit they helped pollinate!

CACTUS FLOWERS

19

The World's OLDEST Plants

GREAT BASIN BRISTLECONE PINE

The prize for oldest living individual plant specimen goes to a North American Great Basin bristlecone pine, which was measured by **ring count** to be 5,064 years old!

There is another plant that some consider even older than the bristlecone pine. Its name is Pando, Latin for "I spread." What started out as a single quaking aspen tree reproduced by **cloning** itself over and over again for thousands of years. Today, it looks like 106 acres of individual trees above the soil, each only about 130 years young. But underground, it's actually a single living organism with a shared root system that is about 80,000 years old.

The scientific method of dating a tree by counting the colored bands in its trunk is called **dendrochronology**. By analyzing a tree's growth rings, scientists know not only how long the tree lived, but also about the environment around the tree during the entire time it was alive. Thanks to dendrochronology, scientists are able to pinpoint major events in a tree's life, down to the calendar year!

TREES COVERED IN MOSS

Moss, hornworts, and liverworts are in a group called **bryophytes**. They are among the oldest and smallest members of the plant kingdom, and have been on Earth more than 450 million years—that's 50 million years longer than ferns, and 230 million years older than the oldest dinosaurs!

Unlike larger plants, bryophytes don't have **vascular** tissues, meaning they don't have a way to transport water and nutrients inside themselves. Like **algae**, they have no roots or stems. But their small size keeps them close to the ground, their primary source of food.

There are about 14,500 **species** of mosses, found all around the world.

CRAZY BUT TRUE

Mosses have an unusual ability to dry out without dying. They actually survive in a state of suspended animation until wet again! When water returns to their habitat, mosses rehydrate in a matter of seconds and become instantly active.

Imagine pouring water on a mummy and having it come back to life!

MOSS: SINGULAR OR PLURAL?

When you look down at a patch of moss, it looks like one plant. In fact, early **botanists**, or scientists who study plants, used to see it that way, too. But we now know that even a small patch of moss is actually hundreds—if not thousands!—of individual plants.

While it's commonly accepted to refer to the entire patch as "moss," it would be more accurate to say "mosses."

MOSS SPORES

Bryophytes don't produce flowers, and they don't produce seeds, either. To reproduce, mosses release **spores**, single-celled bodies much, much smaller than seeds, which grow into new tiny plants.

MOSS GROWING ON TREES

FASTER THAN A SPEEDING BULLET?

Check this out! The fastest land animal, a cheetah, can go from 0 to 75 miles an hour in about 3 seconds, faster than all but the fastest sports cars. As the peregrine falcon dives, it reaches speeds of 242 miles per hour, making it the fastest of all animals. But in terms of acceleration, one **fungus** has them both beat.

PEREGRINE FALCON

CHEETAH

The dung cannon fungus, also called the hat thrower, shoots its **spores** like a rocket, accelerating from 0 to 45 miles per hour instantly!

As the name suggests, the dung cannon fungus grows in cow dung! The mature fungus shoots its spores into clean grass that other cows eat. The spores survive in the animal's digestive tract, making their way into fresh cow patties, where the fungus feeds until it's ready to reproduce.

A Fungus Among Us!

Though sometimes mistaken for plants, mushrooms are actually the fruiting bodies of **fungi**. Fungi belong to a separate kingdom of living things entirely, though they share many characteristics with plants.

There are at least $100,000$ **species** of fungi!

70 to 90% of plants on Earth have a **symbiotic** relationship with fungi.

Caution! Like plants, some mushrooms are edible and others are quite poisonous. There are even mushrooms toxic enough to kill humans! And some of the world's most deadly mushrooms look alarmingly similar to edible varieties.

This Tree Has Taken a Lichen . . .

LICHEN

Though they sometimes look a lot like moss, lichens are actually made up of many organisms such as **fungi**, green **algae**, and cyanobacteria. Similar to how many individual "mosses" can form a single patch, these very different organisms work together **symbiotically** to form a single "composite organism."

CRAZY BUT TRUE

While the algae part of lichens can all be found on their own in nature, the same isn't true for the fungi part of the team. The vast majority of lichen fungi can't survive on their own, and therefore don't grow alone in the wild.

LICHENOMETRY

Lichens grow at a fairly predictable rate, are quick to establish themselves on newly exposed surfaces, and are rarely eaten by insects or animals. That's why lichens can be used as a way of estimating the age of exposed rocks.

This practice, called lichenometry, is especially useful when determining the age of surfaces less than 500 years old, when radiocarbon-dating techniques are less precise.

CRAZY BUT TRUE

Glacier National Park in Montana is home to lichens that have been estimated to be more than 8,600 years old!

WANNA DATE?

Lichens have been used to estimate the age of statues on Easter Island, stone walls in England, and sea-level changes around the world.

EASTER ISLAND

Pollen tube ———

Stamen — Anther ———
Filament ———

Ovule ———

Petal ———

Sepal ———

Receptacle ———

Pedicel —

Stigma

Pistil

Style

Ovary

A flower contains both male and female parts. The male **stamen** consists of a **pollen**-containing **anther** held on a **filament**. The female **pistil** consists of the **stigma**, which receives the pollen, and the **ovary**, the primary reproductive organ, connected by a tube called a **style**. The ovary contains **ovules**, the cells that become the seeds when a flower is fertilized. The ovary itself is what becomes the fruit.

WOLFFIA

A type of duckweed known as *Wolffia* is the smallest of all flowering plants. Sometimes called watermeal, these water plants float like specks of cornmeal on the surface of the water. Individual specimens are small enough to fit through the eye of a needle!

CRAZY BUT TRUE

In case you were wondering, the smallest flowering plant also has the smallest flowers—and the smallest fruit, for that matter. *Wolffia*'s fruit is roughly the size of a grain of table salt!

THE smallest FLOWERING PLANT

There are more than $20{,}000$ **species** of edible plants, including more than $1{,}700$ varieties of edible fruits, $1{,}300$ edible **seeds**, $1{,}100$ edible roots, and 680 edible flowers! There are plants with edible stems, leaves, nectar, **pollen**, sap, and even bark.

INCREDIBLE, EDIBLE PLANTS!

Most of the plants harvested for human consumption have evolved to make their fruits delicious and nutritious so that animals (and people) will spread their seeds.

RECORD-BREAKING FRUITS AND VEGETABLES!

THE WORLD'S LARGEST!
The largest fruit on record
is a pumpkin in 2014 that
weighed 2,323 pounds!

WORLD'S HEAVIEST PRODUCE:

Watermelon:
268 lbs. 13 oz.

Green cabbage:
138 lbs. 4 oz.

Sweet potato:
81 lbs. 9 oz.

Radish:
68 lbs. 9 oz.

Red cabbage:
42 lbs.

Turnip:
39 lbs. 3 oz.

Broccoli:
35 lbs.

Cauliflower:
31 lbs. 4 oz.

Carrot:
18 lbs. 16. oz.

Onion:
18 lbs. 12 oz.

Lemon:
11 lbs. 10 oz.

Tomato:
7 lbs. 12 oz.

Mango:
7 lbs. 9 oz.

Pear:
6 lbs. 8 oz.

Apple:
4 lbs. 1 oz.

Peach:
1 lb. 10 oz.

Fig:
10 oz.

Green pepper:
10 oz.

Strawberry:
8 oz.

Cherry:
0.76 oz.

Blueberry:
0.4 oz.

THE SCIENCE OF DECAY

Unlike plants, which can make their own food through **photosynthesis**, **fungi** feed on the world around them.

Decay is an essential process and is crucial to human survival. Fungi help return materials back into the environment by releasing **enzymes** that break down compounds into nutrients that can be absorbed.

CRAZY BUT TRUE

Fungi are primarily responsible for returning 85 billion tons of carbon back into the atmosphere each year, all in the form of carbon dioxide.

CARNIVOROUS PLANTS

Many plants can't survive on **photosynthesis** alone, requiring nutrients not provided by their environments. Some plants have developed unusual strategies to get what they need—including eating animals!

VENUS FLYTRAP

Plants like the Venus flytrap have hairlike triggers that allow them to catch and digest insects. They do this while the insects are still alive!

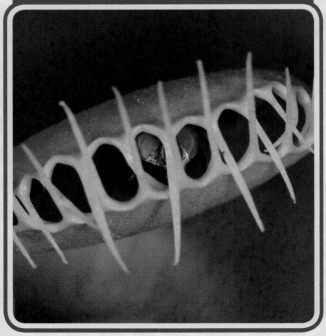

PITCHER PLANT

Others, like the pitcher plant, have modified leaves filled with liquid that trap and dissolve their prey.

CAPE SUNDEW

The Cape sundew has leaves with brightly colored tentacles that release a sticky substance. When a bug gets stuck, the leaf rolls up around it like a boa constrictor!

Fungi can be carnivorous as well. The fungus of the oyster mushroom, for example, feeds on nematode worms by catching them in lasso-like loops when they pass through!

The LARGEST Living Thing

The mushroom is the most recognizable part of a **fungus**. It often has an umbrella-like **cap** that grows on a fleshy stem. **Gills** on the underside of the cap release **spores**, allowing the fungus to reproduce.

MYCELIA

But the much bigger part of a fungus grows underground. **Mycelia**, the rootlike structures that feed the fungus, often take the form of microscopic threads, invisible to the naked eye. Yet the mycelia of some fungi extend enormous distances, sometimes stretching for miles.

The largest known fungus is one of the kind called the honey fungus. It is more than 2,000 years old. Over the course of its lifetime, it has threaded its way through more than 2,384 acres of forest soil in the Blue Mountains of eastern Oregon. It is considered the largest single organism alive on the planet!

Best Fronds Forever

FEATHER PLANTS

Ferns, along with horsetails, clubmosses, spikemosses, and quillworts, are considered **pteridophytes**, or feather plants. These plants are **vascular**, meaning they have **xylem** and **phloem** tissues that transport water and nutrients internally. But unlike most vascular plants, pteridophytes don't produce flowers or **seeds**; instead, they reproduce via **spores**.

There are about $13,000$ known pteridophyte **species**, including $12,000$ varieties of fern. They live all over the world, from the tropics to polar regions. There are ground ferns, floating ferns, hanging ferns, poisonous ferns, iridescent and colorful ferns, and ferns as big as trees.

CLUBMOSSES

FERNS

HORSETAILS

SPIKEMOSSES

49

CRAZY BUT TRUE

A fern is responsible for the world's first terrariums—and all by accident! In 1829, a single fern **spore** made its way into a glass bottle. Nathaniel Bagshaw Ward, a scientist studying insects at the time, discovered the resulting young plant and noticed how the bottle held in moisture as the plant breathed. Soon after, "Wardian cases" took Victorian England by storm and revolutionized the long-distance transport of living plants throughout the world.

TRUE OR FALSE?

People used to think that ferns were magic.

ANSWER: **True!** Up until fairly recently, people didn't understand how ferns reproduced without flowers, fruits, or **seeds**. Many cultures gave the plants mystical significance. It wasn't until 1794 that spores were discovered, when a British surgeon in Jamaica named John Lindsay bragged that he'd managed to grow baby ferns from "dust."

Can You Guess a Dinosaur's Favorite Tree?

GINKGO TREES

Frankly, they didn't have as many choices as we do today. Many of the trees we know and love didn't exist 200 million years ago, when the dinosaurs roamed the Earth. But ginkgo trees did! We know because their leaf imprints have been found in **fossils** from the Jurassic period of the Mesozoic era, and even earlier.

OAK TREE

A relative of ferns, ginkgo trees have been around for 250 million years. They make even a mighty old oak tree seem young by comparison (oaks have been around for only about 85 million years).

WATCH THAT GRASS GROW!

Because of their roots, some grasses are particularly good at combating soil erosion. Marram grass, also called beach grass, is found almost exclusively on coastal sand dunes, where it thrives by holding on to loose, wind-blown soil. Talk about a grassroots attempt!

Grasses cover almost one third of the area of Earth, and about half the area of the United States.

There are approximately 10,000 **species** of grasses, from the kind seen on baseball fields to sugarcane.

Turf grasses are used for lawns, recreational spaces, and urban planning. There are roughly 46,080 blades of grass per square foot of baseball turf (and roughly 5 billion in an entire baseball field). That's a lot of grass!

Not all grass is green. Some grasses are black, blue, brown, red—even silver. And some grasses have multiple colors!

WATER PLANTS

CHALLENGE YOURSELF!

TRUE OR FALSE?
Prehistoric aquatic plants are believed to have been among the first to flower.

ANSWER: True! The first flowers were probably on water plants. Scientists have found fossils that look somewhat like early water lilies.

WATER LILIES

Truly aquatic plants are called **hydrophytes**. They have flat leaves and air sacs that enable them to float. Their roots are made to take in oxygen from the water. And many of the parts of plants that prevent water loss in land plants aren't present.

TRUE OR FALSE?
Water plants don't have leaves.

ANSWER: False! In fact, the record holder for the largest undivided leaves in the world is an aquatic plant. The giant Amazon water lily has enormous circular leaves, some of which are more than 8.5 feet across!

FLOATING PADS

AMAZON WATER LILY

GLOW-IN-THE-DARK ALGAE

On the Cambodian island of Koh Rong, where we shot two seasons of *Survivor*, there is even glow-in-the-dark **algae**! At night, you can spot algae on the beach that are **bioluminescent**, meaning they can produce their own light. When you take a boat ride at night or go into the water with a snorkel, the water lights up. There are reports of colonies of algae in the Indian Ocean large enough that you could read this book by the light they emit!

SINGULAR MICROSCOPIC ALGAE

Super-Small: Though most often too small to be seen with the naked eye, **algae** can be found nearly anywhere there is both sunlight and water—even only a drop!

ALGAE SURVIVAL

Hyper-Resilient: Algae can live in both freshwater and salt water. Some types of algae can even survive in boiling hot temperatures, such as in hot springs. Others not only survive but thrive in snow and even polar conditions.

RED ALGAE

Healing Powers:
Red algae have natural antiviral properties and a great many medical applications. They enhance the body's immune system and are used to combat cold sores, weight gain, and high cholesterol. They are also used to fight diseases like asthma, urinary tract infections, stomach disorders, and more.

RED TIDE

Chemical Weapons: Algae are equipped to transform sunlight into food. But when nutrients are sparse, golden algae can actually become toxic enough to kill fish and competing algae. Another type of algae produces a poisonous phenomenon called red tide, which can kill marine fish, birds, and mammals. It can even harm people!

A Serious Threat!

SPOTTED KNAPWEED

Spotted knapweed is an **invasive species** of plant with a **taproot** that can suck up water faster than its neighbors. Scientists also suspect it is **allelopathic**, meaning it poisons the ground so other plants won't grow. And since it tastes bad, few insects or animals will eat it.

Spotted knapweed covers millions of acres of the western United States. It is particularly threatening for ranchers, as it rapidly replaces the plants cattle and other livestock graze on. Battling knapweed costs ranchers in Montana millions of dollars each year.

Luckily, spotted knapweed has many natural enemies, including insects whose favorite food is knapweed flowers. And without the flowers, the plants can't reproduce. By introducing the bugs to lands plagued by knapweed, ranchers hope one day to eliminate the invasive species from their land.

Each knapweed plant can produce up to 18,000 **seeds**. And each seed can remain **dormant** for 5 years, waiting for the perfect conditions to germinate.

INVASIVE SPECIES!

ENGLISH IVY

Colonists brought English ivy to the United States in the early 1700s. It is an **evergreen**, cold-hardy, and fast-growing ground cover, still popular in landscape design. But its aggressive growth kills trees and carries plant diseases.

JAPANESE HONEYSUCKLE

Japanese honeysuckle was first brought to Long Island, New York, in 1806, and can now be found up and down the East Coast. An aggressive, smothering vine, honeysuckle has few natural enemies in North America, allowing it to outcompete native plant **species**.

PURPLE LOOSESTRIFE

Purple loosestrife was brought to the United States from Europe in the 1800s. Valued for its showy flowers and medicinal uses, the plant now grows aggressively in all the contiguous states (except for Florida), where it can rapidly take over wetland areas. Each plant can produce as many as 2 million **seeds** per year.

KUDZU

Kudzu was brought to the United States by Japan for the first official world's fair in 1876. It was promoted as a way to control erosion. The Soil Conservation Service planted a million acres of kudzu in the 1930s and '40s before realizing how aggressive the plant could be, growing up to a foot a day.

THE FLOWER INDUSTRY

As popular as flowers have always been, scientists didn't understand how to artificially **pollinate** flowers themselves until the twentieth century. Today, there's a whole science dedicated to breeding flowers, which is called **floriculture**.

In the United States, people buy 10 million flowers a day! And perfumes made with flowers are a worldwide industry worth $30 billion annually.

Ancient Egyptians placed cut flowers in vases for decoration, and used them in ceremonies and burials. Ancient Greeks made garlands and wreaths. Ancient Romans decorated with roses at mealtime, and held banquets where rose petals rained down from above. In ancient China, flowers were placed on altars and depicted in paintings.

California grows more fresh flowers than any other state, providing the United States with more than 75% of its flower crops. But imported flowers still account for more than half of the flowers sold in the United States. Colombia, in South America, accounts for more than 75% of fresh flower imports to the United States.

COMING UP ROSES!

ROSES

There are more than 100 **species** of roses, and countless **hybrids** (the offspring of two different species of plants) ranging from tiny bushes to 50-foot plants requiring external support. At least 20,000 hybrids have been developed in the last 150 years alone. In fact, it has been estimated that new **cultivars** are introduced every day!

More than 1.5 billion cut roses are bought annually in the United States.

Today, one fluid ounce of the world's most expensive perfume calls for 28 dozen roses!

Rose hips, the flower's fruit, are rich in vitamin C and bioflavonoids, and are a good source of vitamins A, B, E, and K. They contain calcium, iron, manganese, magnesium, phosphorus, potassium, and zinc. Rose hips are said to stimulate the immune system and reduce fever. They also have anti-inflammatory, astringent, antiseptic, antioxidant, and decongestant properties.

Caution: Romantic but deadly!
While all roses are edible, and in fact nutritious, the pesticides used on store-bought roses are toxic! For your safety, make sure to eat only roses free of chemicals!

ROSES

ORCHID FACTS

During the Victorian era (roughly 1838 to 1910), orchids were so expensive that explorers would risk their lives hunting for them. It was a dangerous venture, from gathering **species** to interacting with indigenous peoples, but the right specimen could sell for serious money.

CHALLENGE YOURSELF!

Which familiar flavor comes from an orchid?

A Honey   **C** Vanilla

B Cinnamon   **D** Chocolate

ANSWER: C!
Vanilla extract is made from the seedpods of the vanilla orchid.

Orchids come in every possible color— except for one. Which color is it?

CHALLENGE YOURSELF!

ANSWER: Black. There are no known species of black orchids—or any truly black-petaled flowers, for that matter.

ORCHID

73

Oh, Christmas Tree

Between 25 and 30 million Christmas trees are sold in the United States every year, and each takes an average of 7 years to grow. Some **species** take as many as 15 years to grow.

Christmas trees are usually some type of fir, pine, or spruce tree. Today, there are approximately 350 million Christmas trees growing on 15,000 farms in all 50 states, covering about 350,000 acres of land.

Christmas trees can be the natural homes of a great variety of animals. A red tree vole, which is a type of rodent, can spend its entire life in a single Christmas tree!

The tallest Douglas fir tree (a type of Christmas tree) alive today lives in Coos County, Oregon. It is 327 feet tall! Who wants to put on that tree topper?!

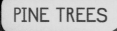

PINE TREES

WISTERIA HOUSE, SIERRA MADRE

According to *Guinness World Records*, the largest blossoming plant in existence is a single wisteria (also spelled wistaria) vine in Sierra Madre, California; it covers more than an acre and produces more than 1.5 million blooms.

Planted in 1894, the vine was 96 years old and weighed 250 tons when it entered *Guinness World Record*s in 1990. Now it is more than 120 years old, and the vine in bloom is stronger than ever! The Wisteria House has even been dubbed one of the 7 horticultural wonders of the world!

CRAZY BUT TRUE

A woman named Alice Brugman bought the vine for 75 cents. Now, it's being compared to the gardens of Buckingham Palace, the Taj Mahal, Mexico's Floating Gardens, and the giant redwood forest in Sequoia National Park!

BUCKINGHAM PALACE

TAJ MAHAL

MEXICO'S FLOATING GARDENS

SEQUOIA NATIONAL PARK

TOMATOES

CHALLENGE YOURSELF!

What is a clue to help you tell a fruit from a vegetable?

A It has seeds.

B It tastes sweet.

C It's brightly colored.

ANSWER: A! Technically speaking, a "fruit" is a fleshy container for **seeds**. Therefore, if there are seeds in what you're eating, it's a fruit. That's right—cucumbers, squash, pumpkins, and green beans are all technically fruits, no matter what the cafeteria lady says!

NO MATTER HOW YOU SLICE IT

There are more than $1,600$ fruits around the world that the average person will never eat. And many of them are so delicious that people travel hundreds or thousands of miles for a taste!

DURIAN FRUIT

Many people claim the durian fruit, grown mainly in Southeast Asia, smells like rotting onions. Others say it smells like sewage! It stinks so badly, in fact, that it's banned from public transportation and some buildings. And yet those who eat it love the taste, which has been described as a "rich custard" with almond flavoring.

PEANUT BUTTER FRUIT

Can you believe there is such a thing as peanut butter fruit? And it actually tastes like peanut butter! There's even a blackberry jam fruit. Eat them together, and maybe they'll taste like peanut butter and jelly!

ICE CREAM BEAN

The South American ice cream bean is named after its sweet flavor and smooth texture. It's so sweet and the fruit's flesh is so soft that some say it should be called the cotton candy bean!

CRAZY BUT TRUE

Durian fruit is so beloved in parts of the world that during its peak season families will camp out under trees to be sure the fruit isn't stolen by neighbors when it falls.

EXUTIC FRUITS

One of my favorite fruits actually comes from Hawaii, and if you can find them you must try them, because they are "miracle berries." They actually alter the way you taste things. For instance, if you were to eat a slice of lemon, it would taste really sour, right? But if you were to eat a miracle berry first and then eat the lemon, the lemon would taste like lemonade! For real! It's so much fun to do! Its official name is *Synsepalum dulcificum*, and when you eat the fruit, it makes other foods taste sweet. You can sometimes find them in grocery stores, or better yet they're easy to grow yourself. Then you could really blow your friends' minds!

TASTE THE WORLD!

Many exotic fruits can be found at specialty stores, including rambutan, lychee, jackfruit, passion fruit, mangosteen, dragon fruit, and African cucumber!

RAMBUTAN

JACKFRUIT

DRAGON FRUIT

AFRICAN CUCUMBER

RHUBARB

You might think poisonous plants are never sold in grocery stores. But you'd be wrong! Rhubarb, for example, is a sweet and tart springtime plant whose stalks are used in pies and other desserts. Yet its leaves are toxic enough to have resulted in human deaths.

APPLE SEEDS

Apple **seeds** are toxic. So are the pits of cherries, apricots, and peaches. In fact, these seeds all contain cyanide, a strong toxin. But don't worry too much. It would take a full measuring cup of ground-up apple seeds to deliver enough cyanide to kill a person.

The peel of a mango fruit contains urushiol, the same allergen that's in poison ivy!

Believe it or not, both lima beans and kidney beans are naturally toxic. They contain dangerous amounts of poisonous compounds when raw, though properly cooked beans are safe. (Phew!)

NUTMEG

A common household spice, nutmeg is usually consumed in very small amounts. But larger doses can cause dehydration, nausea, and serious convulsions. There has even been one death attributed to the spice.

OLEANDER

Oleander is a flowering shrub that can be found all over the United States, especially in southern and western regions. But it's also one of the world's most deadly plants! Its leaves, flowers, and fruit are all poisonous enough to kill a human being.

Many flowers are surprisingly poisonous, including blossoms of the plants lily of the valley, wolfsbane, nightshade, conium, datura, and the famous angel's trumpet. Eating these flowers can lead to all kinds of terrible symptoms, from nausea and hallucinations to paralysis and death.

SUICIDE TREE

Seeds of the suicide tree might be less toxic overall, but spices can disguise the taste of their poison. And unlike other poisons, the symptoms of this plant's toxin are easily mistaken for heart failure. Forensic toxicologists have estimated that people have used the suicide tree more than any other plant to commit murder!

CASTOR OIL PLANT

The seeds of the castor oil plant contain ricin, an incredibly toxic chemical. Swallowing the seeds can lead to mouth sores and bloody diarrhea. Eat as many as four of the seeds, and the plant is likely to kill you. In fact, the plant has been named the most poisonous plant in the world by *Guinness World Records*.

AUTUMN CROCUS

The autumn crocus is also incredibly poisonous. The flower can cause immediate cardiac arrest, killing a human in minutes. And unlike the other flowers listed here, this flower's poison has no known antidote!

Plants as Medicine

NIGHTSHADE BERRIES

Many of the same toxic chemicals in plants that make them dangerous can, in the right hands, be put to use as medicine. Deadly nightshade berries, for example, contain atropine, which is used in medicine to stop muscular spasms and to relax the eye for surgery.

Between 50,000 and 80,000 plants are used medicinally. Of the top 150 prescription drugs available in the United States, about 74% come from plants.

In the United States, at least 30,000 people are saved each year by anticancer drugs made from plants.

Around the world, there are populations of people that do not have access to store-bought drugs. Many still use natural plant remedies to fight illness and combat pain, including applications of plants that are poisonous, even deadly, in large enough doses.

DANGER! RAZOR GRASS!

Ever heard of razor grass? There are several **species** of grass that have leaves sharp enough to cut you simply by brushing against them. Cuts from razor grass sting like paper cuts, and they often itch or become inflamed.

Pampas grass, a large South American grass that is sometimes used decoratively in the United States, is one type of razor grass. Tufts of the grass are typically 12 feet tall, with the leaves spilling outward like a fountain. Each 10-foot-long blade is only a half-inch thick, but razor sharp.

PAMPAS GRASS

BAMBOO

Technically a giant type of grass, bamboo grows faster than any other plant in the world. Certain **species** can grow up to almost 3 feet per day (!) and reach heights of almost 100 feet in a single growing season.

One and a half billion people use, eat, or trade bamboo around the world. A fast-growing building material, bamboo is durable enough to replace wood for many applications. It's used to make skateboards, surfboards, snowboards—even bamboo bicycles!

Many varieties of bamboo are considered invasive. Their underground roots can spread as far as **20 feet,** worming their way under barriers only to pop up as new plants on the other side.

Bamboo is so strong that it is used for construction scaffolding in places like India, Bangladesh, Sri Lanka, and Indonesia. It was even used as scaffolding during the building of the Great Wall of China!

By some measures, dried bamboo is stronger than steel! In many island countries where we shoot *Survivor*, the locals actually make their own thick bamboo nails and use them for constructing homes.

Slow Blooms

AGAVE FLOWER

The agave plant is sometimes called the century plant because of how long it can take to bloom. The agave plant flowers only once in its lifetime, sometimes 60 years or more.

Agave plants' flowers don't have much of a scent. That's why they are **pollinated** by birds, which don't have a very good sense of smell. Instead, agave plants spend their energy growing a huge stalk, so hummingbirds are more likely to spot their flowers far across the desert.

SAGUARO CACTUS

Generally speaking, cacti are the slowest plants to grow. One **species** of cactus, the saguaro, grows only a single inch in the first 10 years of its life. It doesn't branch until after its 16th birthday. And it doesn't flower until it's around 60 years old!

QUEEN OF THE NIGHT CACTUS

The Queen of the Night cacti bloom only one night of the year. But they're worth the wait. The plants' white flowers can be as large as a foot wide and smell sweet, reminiscent of vanilla and orange blossoms.

95

SEED LIFE

TRUE OR FALSE?
Seeds can stay viable for hundreds of years.

ANSWER: True! Seeds are built to last hundreds, even thousands of years.

One 2,000-year-old seed, discovered in a clay jar in the 1960s during the archaeological excavation of King Herod's Palace in Jerusalem, successfully sprouted in 2005. It's since been identified as a Judean date palm—a plant that was extinct for centuries, despite its having once been a staple crop there. The palm was named Methuselah, after a character from the Bible said to be the longest-living man. In 2011, Methuselah flowered. As of 2015, Methuselah was 10 feet tall, producing fruit, and even producing offspring.

FENNEL SEEDS

CHIA SEEDS

POMEGRANATE
SEEDS

WHITE SESAME
SEEDS

RIDING ON . . . YOU?

Some plants, like burdock, have **seeds** that use Velcro-like hooks or spurs to stick to fur and fabric. These seeds get carried off accidentally by animals, including humans—usually without their even knowing it. Others are less discreet, with pointy spikes that can stick painfully into an animal's paw. Seeds of the aptly named puncture vine are barbed with spikes sharp and strong enough to penetrate bicycle tires, or even a rubber shoe sole!

Hiking through the Australian outback, I picked up more than my fair share of spiky hitchhikers. In fact, after one particularly long trek my socks were so tangled with barbed seeds that I couldn't pick them all out. I had to throw my favorite socks away!

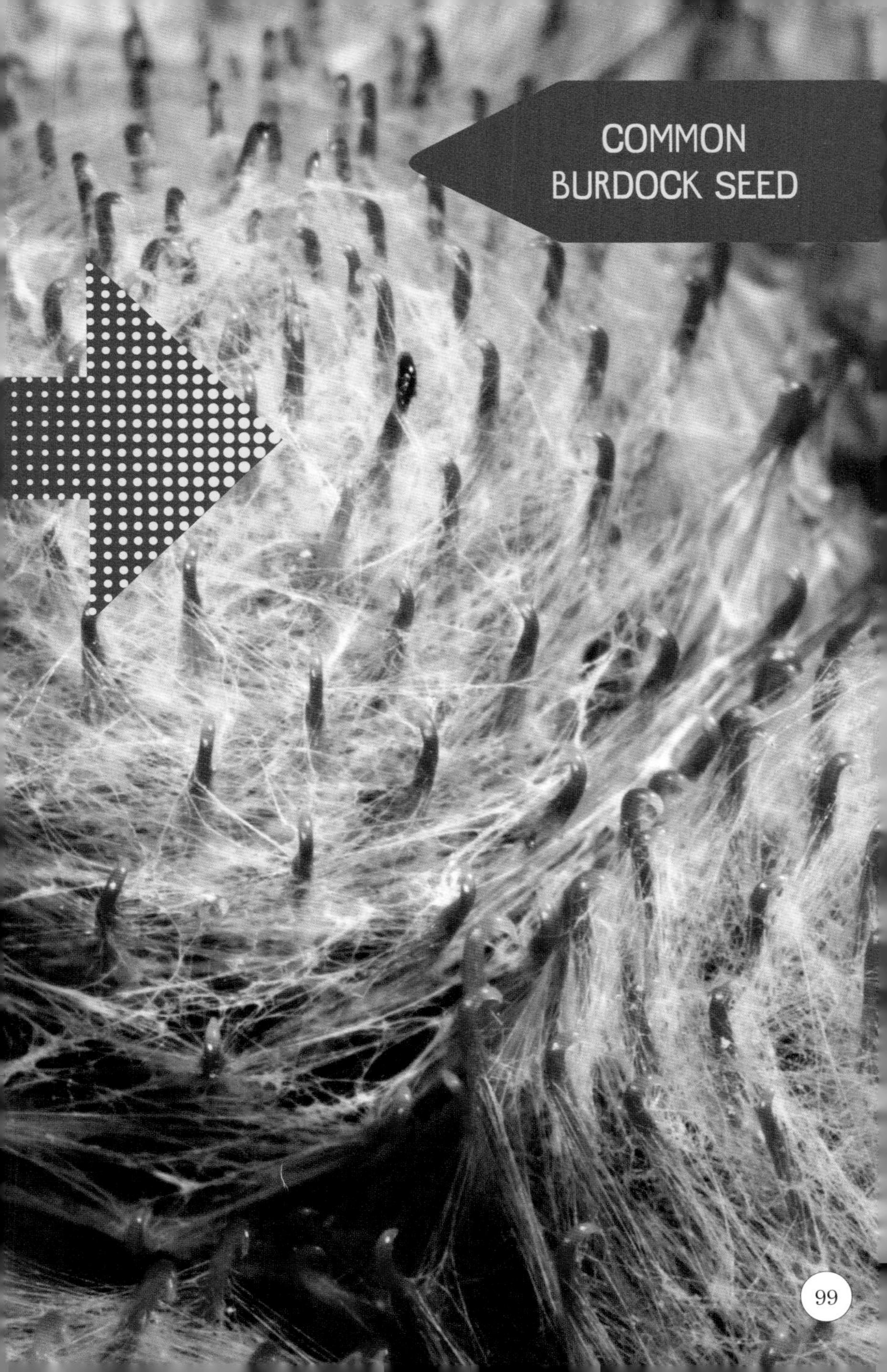
COMMON
BURDOCK SEED

CRAZY BUT TRUE

MOBILE SEEDS

More **seeds** travel by catching a ride with animals than by any other means. And most of those don't ride outside, on an animal's fur, but *inside*, in an animal's digestive system. When an animal poops, the seeds of the fruit it has eaten come out and are deposited onto the ground—often far away from where they were swallowed.

ZEBRA

DEER

Watch your step! These seeds travel with their own built-in fertilizer!

DANGEROUS SEEDS

Perhaps the most ferocious spiked seed belongs to the South African grapple plant. Its seedcase is nicknamed the devil's claw and has a dozen crippling hooks, capable of cutting into nearly any foot, including those of hoofed animals. There are reports of lions having died after encountering these dangerous seeds!

GRAPPLE SEED

RIDING ON WIND:

Some plants have specialized **seeds** adapted to take to the air. Dandelion seeds, for example, come equipped with individual parachutes that help them ride the wind to far-flung soils. Maple trees and pines have winged seeds that spin through the air like tiny helicopters. But the Javan cucumber vine might have them all beat. Each of its seeds has two 5-inch paper-thin wings that allow it to glide super far. These amazing seeds reportedly inspired the design of early aircraft! No wonder, since they can travel several hundred feet through the forest before making their way to the ground.

DANDELION

RIDING ON WATER:

Plants that grow near water often have seeds adapted to float. Coconuts, for example, sprout once they wash up on shore. Other plants that grow in water, such as lotuses, have seeds that eventually sink. But a mangrove tree's seeds begin to germinate while still attached to the parent plant. The seedlings are only cast into the ocean after they are about a foot long. And then they float upright in the water, partially weighed down by the seed.

MANGROVE
SEEDLINGS

103

Follow That
Moss!

TRUE OR FALSE?
Moss grows only on the north side of trees.

ANSWER: **False!** Moss can grow anywhere there is sufficient shade and moisture. But it's true that in the Northern Hemisphere more sun shines on the south side of trees than on the north. Therefore, if one side of trees is mossier than the other, it is likely the north side. In the Southern Hemisphere, the opposite is true. So if you're ever lost in the woods and need to find your bearings, moss really can help!

Fungus Medicine

Fungus has saved the lives of millions of people around the world.

PENICILLIUM FUNGUS

Considered among the most important medical break-throughs in modern history, the discovery of **antibiotics** changed the way people fight illnesses and diseases. And it all started with one lucky **spore** of *Penicillium* fungus.

In 1928, a Scottish scientist named Alexander Fleming left a petri dish of Staphylococci **bacteria** uncovered in his lab. He later noticed that all of the bacteria, which can cause infections, had been killed off by a stray fungus. This happy accident led to the development of penicillin, the world's first antibiotic.

Other fungi have been found to have anticancer and anticholesterol properties. Fungi are used to bolster the immune system and to combat diseases like malaria and diabetes.

ASPIRIN, a common pain reliever, can be made from the bark of a WILLOW TREE.

QUININE, an anti-inflammatory fever reducer used to treat malaria, is found naturally in the bark of a CINCHONA TREE.

MORPHINE, a severe pain reliever, is found in the seedpod of the opium POPPY FLOWER.

DAFFODIL BULBS contain a chemical that is used to treat ALZHEIMER'S DISEASE.

The leaves of an ENGLISH YEW TREE are used in the treatment of BREAST CANCER.

The first medical gloves used by doctors were also made from plants. Latex, a kind of rubber that balloons are often made of, comes from the rubber tree.

COFFEE

TEA

Coffee and tea both contain caffeine, a mild stimulant that also has several medical applications. Caffeine is hands-down the world's most widely consumed drug. About 90% of people around the world consume caffeine every day—70% of which comes in the form of coffee.

CRAZY BUT TRUE

Like all drugs, caffeine is officially poisonous. Drinking too much caffeine can even be lethal! But it would take drinking 100 cups of coffee in a single afternoon to kill a person.

FOOD PLANTS QUIZ!

Which is an example of edible bark?

A Pine tree bark

B Pepper

C Cinnamon

D Oatmeal

ANSWER: **C!** Cinnamon is a spice and flavoring that comes from the inner bark of a tree. It is also used medicinally, as well as in cosmetics and perfume.

What is the only fruit with the seeds on the outside?

(A) Raspberry   (C) Kiwi

(B) Strawberry   (D) Eggplant

ANSWER: **B!** Those small specks on a strawberry fruit are the plant's seeds. Each strawberry carries about 200 of them!

RASPBERRY

STRAWBERRY

KIWI

EGGPLANT

OTHERWORLDLY VEGETABLES?

ROMANESCO
Romanesco looks a little like broccoli from outer space! But, in fact, it's from Italy.

FIDDLEHEADS
Alien tentacles? No. Fiddle-heads are the curled-up baby fronds of a fern.

OKINAWAN SWEET POTATO

Don't be alarmed by the purple color. The Okinawan sweet potato tastes almost exactly like the more familiar orange ones.

WHITE ASPARAGUS

Though it looks different, white asparagus is the same as the green kind, only it's grown entirely in the dark, preventing photosynthesis, and making it more tender.

These Flowers Stink!

Some flowers attract pollinators by smelling **downright awful!**

The flowers of New Guinea's *Bulbophyllum phalaenopsis* smell like rotting mice, specifically! Those of the Caribbean *Aristolochia grandiflora* smell like rotting rats. And *Helicodiceros muscivorus*'s flowers are said to smell like dead horses! As if that wasn't bad enough, their flowers don't open on cool or cloudy days, only on hot sunny ones, so the stink will carry.

ARISTOLOCHIA GRANDIFLORA

CARRION FLOWERS

Carrion flowers release the odor of rotting meat to attract their pollinators—scavenging flies and flesh-eating beetles.

THE CORPSE LILY!

TITAN ARUM FLOWER

The titan arum, or corpse lily, stands 10 feet tall and blooms for only 2 days. But when it does bloom, it smells like a decomposing mammal. And the smell is reportedly strong enough to make a person faint!

EASTERN SKUNK CABBAGE

More than just smelling like a rotting corpse, the large, fragrant **spadix** jutting up from the center actually heats up! Probably to mimic a recently dead body.

Eastern skunk cabbage smells like roadkill skunk. Like the corpse lily, this wetland flower is capable of generating its own heat in order to mimic a dead body.

CHAMPION TREES!

The name Champion Tree is given to the largest known tree in each **species**. The National Register of Big Trees lists every Champion Tree in the continental United States, taking into account trunk circumference, total height, and average crown spread.

Toward the top of their list sits General Sherman, a 275-foot-tall giant sequoia that lives in California's Sequoia National Park. General Sherman is considered the largest single-stem tree on the planet! General Sherman isn't the tallest tree, however.

CRAZY BUT TRUE

In 1902, a very large Douglas fir tree was cut down in Vancouver, British Columbia. It was later reported to measure 415 feet! An even taller Douglas fir was reportedly cut down in Washington in 1897. It was said to measure 465 feet! If either of them hadn't been cut down, one of them might have been named a Champion Tree today.

THE TALLEST TREE ON EARTH!

That title belongs to Hyperion, a coast redwood also in Northern California. It is the tallest living organism on record. Roughly 700 to 800 years old, Hyperion stands 379 feet tall—that's taller than the Statue of Liberty!

THE HARDEST AND HEAVIEST WOOD

CHALLENGE YOURSELF!

TRUE OR FALSE?
All wood floats.

ANSWER: **False!** There are about 30 **species** of trees that produce ironwood, a strong type of wood so heavy that it actually sinks! According to *Guinness World Records*, the tree with the hardest wood in the world is the South African black ironwood, a member of the olive family.

IRONWOOD TREE

Botanical Assassins!

HEMLOCK

Socrates, a famous Greek philosopher, was executed in 399 BC. He was sentenced to death by drinking hemlock.

HELLEBORE

Almost two centuries earlier, an ancient Greek military alliance used hellebore to poison the water supply of their enemies.

DEADLY MUSHROOM

Historians now believe that Claudius, an ancient Roman emperor, died after being poisoned by deadly mushrooms.

MONKSHOOD

During World War II, Nazi scientists used monkshood to make poisoned bullets.

RICIN

The Soviet Union used ricin from the seeds of the castor oil plant to stealthily murder its enemies during the Cold War.

Who put the fossil in fossil fuels?

FOSSIL FERNS

Coal is made up largely of fossilized ferns. **360 million years** ago, ferns and other feather plants dominated the landscape. And they continued to do so for at least **100 million years**. After they were buried underground, the immense pressure of the Earth slowly turned the remains of those prehistoric ferns and other organic matter into the prized **fossil** fuels we depend on today.

CRAZY BUT TRUE

Scientists believe some of the earliest **pteridophytes** grew to be much larger than they are now. About a thousand fern **species** still grow to be as large as trees today, some as tall as 33 feet! But it's likely that ancient ferns were even larger still, having few developed plants to compete with.

Some ferns, though, still look exactly as they did millions of years ago. Fossilized fronds of the fern species *Osmunda claytoniana* that were found in Triassic deposits in Antarctica appear to be identical to the same plant today.

Can Pond
Scum Save
the World?

BIOFUEL

Many scientists are concerned with finding sustainable alternatives to **fossil** fuels—which emit unwanted gases into the enviornment. Common pond scum, a type of **algae** also known as cyano-bacteria, is being studied as a potential **biofuel** alternative to gasoline. In fact, scientists at the UK Carbon Trust predict that by 2030 algae-based biofuels could replace gas as we know it.

THE WORLD'S FIRST PAPER

PAPYRUS

Today's paper industry currently uses nearly 4 billion trees each year. But the first paper wasn't made from tree pulp. It was called papyrus, and it was made from an aquatic plant with the same name.

The ancient Egyptians cut the spongy **pith** inside the plant's reed stalks into strips. They flattened them with rollers to get as much water out as possible. Then they laid them out in flat sheets, allowing the edges to overlap—similar to how lasagna noodles are layered in a lasagna dish. The sheets were then pressed flat, weighed down with rocks, and allowed to dry. The sugars in the plant formed a natural glue, fixing the strips in place. The result was a thin sheet of parchment, similar to today's paper, which could be written or drawn on.

PAPYRUS

CASH CROPS

More than 84 million acres of corn are grown every year in the United States. There are also 73.8 million acres of soybeans and 45.7 million acres of wheat grown in the States.

CORNFIELD

Modern industrial agriculture involves **monocultures**, meaning that a single plant **species** is grown over a vast area. Large-scale farming allows food plants to be grown and harvested as cheaply as technologically possible. But it also leaves crops vulnerable to pests and diseases, which can spread far more rapidly without the protections **biodiversity** provides.

The bananas we eat today are in danger! All around the world, farmers grow the exact same kind of banana, called the Cavendish. Up until the 1950s, a different kind of banana, called Big Mike, was sold in stores. It had a different flavor from the bananas we eat today. But a worldwide disease wiped out nearly all of those bananas. And the same disease threatens to wipe out today's bananas, too, which could lead to sudden banana shortages all over the world. And potentially to another new banana, one that tastes different from the banana we eat and love.

CRAZY BUT TRUE

Fewer than 20 species of fruits and vegetables make up more than 90% of the food eaten in the United States. That's only .1% of the edible plants available.

YELLOW TULIP WITH BULB

Many of the world's favorite spring flowers grow from bulbs, including tulips, daffodils, lilies, and hyacinths. These flowers provide some of the first colors each spring.

Bulbs store moisture and nutrients during the winter. In the spring, this stored moisture allows them to grow into flowers more quickly than other plants. Their early shoots and leaves race to capture and store sunlight for the following year while other plants have yet to produce their first spring leaves.

CRAZY BUT TRUE

Some of the foods we eat are actually the bulbs of flowering plants! Examples include onions, garlic, and shallots.

GARLIC

ONIONS

BLOSSOMS & BULBS

TULIPS

CRAZY BUT TRUE

During Holland's "tulip mania," bulbs of the flowers were so expensive that they could be used as money! In 1637, at the height of the craze, the most expensive tulips (known as Viceroys) were being sold for more than 10 times what some people made in a whole year.

Gerbera daisies were discovered in South Africa in 1884. They are also native to Asia and South America.

GERBERA DAISIES

RAFFLESIA ARNOLDII

Southeast Asia's "Big Flower" smells like death. The jungle flowers of the plant *Rafflesia arnoldii* can grow to be about three feet wide, making them the largest single blooms of any flower! (The titan arum, like a sunflower, is actually many small flowers.)

CRAZY BUT TRUE

When the huge flower appears, it's the only visible part of the whole plant. *Rafflesia arnoldii* is a **parasite**, meaning it lives off a host plant. It has no stem or leaves; instead, it has only rootlike structures that attach and hide inside the tissues of host vines.

LIVING ROCK CACTI

Some plants use camouflage to hide from potential threats. Living rock cacti and pebble plants, for example, don't look like ordinary plants. Instead, they have dark geometric leaves that allow them to blend into their surroundings.

LIVING ROCK CACTUS

CACTI

Spines protect cacti from thirsty animals that would otherwise graze on them. They have adapted leaves that act as reservoirs, holding water inside the plant. Some cacti swell when water is available or go into total **dormancy** until the next rain, surviving months or even years of drought.

Caution! Plants!

CACTI WITH GLOCHIDS

Cacti have sharp spines, to keep from getting eaten. But did you know that some can get lodged in an animal's skin, like a splinter or porcupine quill? The fine, hairlike barbs are called **glochids**. They can penetrate with the slightest touch, and once they do they're very hard to remove.

HIMALAYAN BLACKBERRY THORNS

Roses famously have thorns, as does bougainvillea. But the Himalayan black-berry's bite puts them both to shame. Its stalk grows to be 2 inches thick, with inch-long thorns. One plant can cover half an acre with brambles like barbed wire.

GIANT HOGWEED

Poison oak and poison ivy grow nearly all over the United States, especially east of the Rocky Mountains. Contact with any part of either plant can lead to itchy, even painful rashes. But those symptoms are gentle compared to giant hogweed, which works with sunlight to actually burn flesh. A brush with this plant results in purple wounds that leave perma-nent scars!

KELP GROWT

CHALLENGE
YOURSELF!

Does kelp grow quickly or slowly?

ANSWER: **Quickly!** Kelp (a type of seaweed) can grow up to 18 inches per day. These towering aquatic **algae** provide homes and food for thousands of **species** of marine animals.

Kelp grows in cold, nutrient-rich water, including along the West Coast of North America. Because algae require sunlight to survive, kelp rarely grows in water deeper than 130 feet.

CORDYCEPS

Perhaps more extreme than any other carnivorous plant known to man, the *Cordyceps* **fungus** doesn't simply trap its prey. Instead, it uses mind control! An insect infected with this fungus roams around like a zombie, searching for a good place for the mushroom to grow—all while the fungus feeds on its insides! Eventually, the host climbs high up onto a plant and dies. The *Cordyceps* mushroom then grows out of the insect's head, spreading **spores** in all directions.

RAT-EATING PITCHER PLANT

The carnivorous plant with the largest known trap is the Nepenthes rajah, or rat-eating pitcher plant. It's a 15-inch-tall pitcher plant in the Philippines that has a volume of more than three quarters of a gallon. It's big enough to catch mice and even rats!

SHEEP-EATING PITCHER PLANT

On the dry hillsides of Chile is the Puya chilensis, or sheep-eating plant, which has a habit of killing sheep! It grows to be nearly 10 feet tall, and its flowers resemble a medieval mace. When trying to approach the plant's flower, sheep and other animals get tangled in the leaves' hooked spines. Eventually, they die of starvation, and their rotting bodies fertilize the plant.

WEIRD-LOOKING FLOWER!

CEROPEGIA SANDERSONII FLOWER

The parachute flower looks a little like a hairy megaphone. It is also commonly known as the fountain flower or the umbrella plant.

FUNNY FLOWERS

ONCIDIUM HENEKENII

The bee orchid actually looks like a bee! It's **pollinated** by male bees, which mistake the flower for a female bee.

CHALLENGE YOURSELF!

What do you think these flowers look like?

ANSWER: Top left clockwise: Monkey face, Bird, Parrot, and Lips.

DRACULA SIMIA

PHALAENOPSIS

IMPATIENS PSITTACINA

PSYCHOTRIA ELATA

149

Flower Power!

CARNATIONS

Carnations continue to bloom long after they are cut, bolstering their popularity as cut flowers. They are considered the official flower of Mother's Day. Like roses, carnations are edible. In fact, they have been used as a flavoring for liquor, wine, and beer for hundreds of years.

CHRYSANTHEMUMS

Chrysanthemums, also called mums, are in the same composite flower family as sunflowers and gerbera daisies. For these **species**, what appears to be a single flower is actually made up of hundreds of individual flowers! A close look at the center of the "flower" reveals smaller florets, each with its own flower parts.

CRAZY BUT TRUE

Did you know you can actually change the color of white carnations? And it's really easy! Here's all you do. Take a jar of water and add your favorite food coloring. Then place the carnation stems in the jar and let them sit for 4 to 6 hours. That's it! The flowers "drink" the water from the stems all the way up to the petals. They will transform in front of your eyes!

THE LARGEST PINECONE

Of the more than 100 **species** of pines in the world, the largest pinecones belong to California's Coulter pine. They grow to be up to 14 inches long and can weigh more than 8 pounds!

That's equal in size and weight to not just one but two bricks! Now imagine standing under that tree when it starts dropping its pinecones!

Even larger, though, are the **seed** cones of tropical cycads. Their cones can grow to be 3 feet long and can weigh up to 95 pounds!

COULTER PINE

153

Seaweed Ice Cream?! Yuck!

TRUE OR FALSE?
Fish aren't the only ones eating algae. Odds are, you eat algae, too.

ANSWER: **True!** Carrageenan and agar-agar are two common food additives made from red **algae** (Porphyra is one type). They can be found throughout the grocery store in foods like ice cream, yogurt, frozen macaroni-and-cheese dinners, marshmallows, pudding, chocolate milk, some salad dressings, and more!

CRAZY BUT TRUE

In Japan, Porphyra farming alone is a $1 billion industry!

On my travels, I've also eaten seaweed in salads and sushi, as dried chips, and even in pill form. All around the world, algae are farmed as vitamin- and mineral-rich super-foods, including Porphyra, edible kelp, and spirulina.

KELP

In the winter, the ground can freeze, leaving little moisture for plants to absorb. Some plants survive by going **dormant**. But **evergreen** trees stay active in cold longer than most plants, thanks to their needles.

PINE NEEDLES

Desert plants and arctic plants can grow at incredibly slow rates. In fact, a Sitka spruce is believed to have grown only 11 inches in the past 98 years. That's the slowest-growing plant on record!

WHY DO SOME TREES LOSE THEIR LEAVES?

The trees that lose their leaves in winter are called **deciduous**. These plants can tell when winter is coming, and drop their leaves in preparation. The broader leaves of deciduous trees use up a lot of water. By dropping them, the trees are able to stay hydrated during the drier winter months.

Trees' ability to lose their leaves also protects them from winter gusts that might otherwise uproot them if the leaves were still there.

ENDANGERED PLANTS

At least 34,000 of the world's 275,000 plant **species** are in danger of extinction, including 15,000 medicinal plants.

That's one eighth of all plants!

In the United States, 29% of 16,000 plant species are in danger of going extinct.

Of the top 150 prescription drugs sold in the United States, 111 come from plants—many of which were first discovered in rain forests and other at-risk areas. When a plant becomes extinct, we not only lose that plant forever, we also lose the possibility of discovering life-saving cures for the world's deadliest diseases. Sadly, experts estimate that at the current rate of plant extinction, the Earth loses at least one potential major drug every two years.

GLOSSARY

ALGAE: plants without roots that live off nutrients in water

ALLELOPATHY: a biological phenomenon in which one living thing chemically prevents the survival of another

ANGIOSPERMS: plants that have flowers, used for reproduction

ANTHER: the reproductive part of a flower that holds the pollen

ANTIBIOTICS: medicine that destroys or stops the growth of harmful bacteria in the body

BACTERIA: microscopic organisms that are neither plants nor animals, and can cause disease and/or infection

BIODIVERSITY: the variety of life-forms in a given area

BIOFUEL: fuel produced from living things (mostly farmed plants) rather than gathered from deep in the earth

BIOLUMINESCENCE: the ability of a living organism to produce light

BOTANISTS: those who study plants

BRYOPHYTES: plants that lack a vascular system, relying on smaller tissue to distribute water and nutrients internally

CAP: the top of a mushroom, the fruiting part of a fungus

CLONING: a process of producing offspring that are genetically identical to the parent

CULTIVAR: a group of cultivated plants that share the same desired traits

DECIDUOUS: describes plants that shed their leaves, typically in the fall

DENDROCHRONOLOGY: the scientific method of dating trees by counting their growth rings

DORMANCY: a period of time in which an organism becomes inactive

ENZYMES: substances in living things that help trigger biochemical reactions

EVERGREEN: a plant that keeps its leaves year round

FILAMENT: the part of a flower's stamen that holds the anther

FLORICULTURE: the farming of flowers

FOSSIL: remains of a primitive organism, in the form of either a preserved body part or an impression or mold

FUNGUS/FUNGI: an organism that produces spores and feeds on surrounding organic matter

GILL: the underside of a mushroom's cap, which holds reproductive spores

GLOCHIDS: hairlike spines or barbs on a cactus

GYMNOSPERMS: seed-bearing plants that reproduce without forming flowers

HYBRID: the offspring of two different plant species

HYDROPHYTE: a plant that grows submerged in water

INVASIVE SPECIES: a non-native plant or animal whose rapid reproduction hurts the environment

MONOCULTURE: the cultivation of a single crop in a large area

MYCELIA: the underground, rootlike structures of a fungus

OVARY: the part of a flower that turns into a fruit when fertilized

OVULE: the part of a flower that turns into a seed when fertilized

PARASITE: an organism that lives on or in another living thing, often at the expense of the host

PHLOEM: specialized tissue in plants that carries sugars and other nutrients within the plant

PHOTOSYNTHESIS: the process through which plants turn sunlight into chemical energy, usually in the form of sugars

PISTIL: the reproductive part of a flower that collects pollen and contains the ovary

PITH: soft or spongy tissue in plants, often used to store a plant's nutrition

POLLEN: the powdery substance created by the male structure of a flower for fertilization

POLLINATION: the process by which pollen is transferred to the female structure of a flower

PRIMORDIAL: existing in the earliest stage of development

PTERIDOPHYTES: vascular plants that reproduce through seed-like units called spores

RING COUNT: the number of growth rings on a tree, visible when looking at a cross section

SEED: the fertilized ovule of a plant that can grow into a new plant

SPADIX: small flowers embedded in a fleshy stem at the center of an inflorescence (the flowering part of a plant)

SPECIES: a group of living things that have similar characteristics and are able to reproduce

SPORES: very small reproductive units, released from the undersides of ferns and mushrooms instead of seeds

STAMEN: the male reproductive structure of a flower

STIGMA: the reproductive part of the flower that receives pollen

STYLE: the female reproductive structure of a flower

SYMBIOTIC: describes diverse organisms that live together and benefit each other

TAPROOT: a root growing straight down from the stem of a plant into the ground, from which smaller roots emerge

VASCULAR: containing internal vessels used for carrying liquid

XYLEM: specialized tissue in plants that carries water and fluids within a plant

INDEX
Numbers in *italics* refer to illustrations